Spirituality 4 Kids

Discover the Real You...

It Was there all along!

Serena Gaefke

ISBN: 978-0-9972206-3-6

Printed in the United States of America

MERU PRESS®
P.O. Box 277
Livingston, Montana 59047 USA
Visit: **MeruPress.org**
Email: info@MeruPress.org

For additional copies and more information,
visit: **HeartsCenter.org**

Also available at:
Amazon.com

Contents

That's quite a line up!

Yeah, I wish I had teachings like that when I was a pup.

Dedication

To the young people of today, curious about their spirituality.

To the young people of today, seeking higher truth.

To the young people of today, who desire to live life to the fullest, discover themselves and the meaning of it all.

May you find answers, inspiration and more in this book!

CH 1: Who are you? A journey in God-Self discovery

<u>Long, long ago</u>
One day, a long, long time ago, longer than you can even imagine, there was only God. And out of this God, there came many drops, many pearls, many sparkles of light across the ocean of God's being. One of them, was you.

"Who am I," you ask? A son of God, or daughter too. It is you, through and through! No worldly image you do fit, but here as you do read and sit, I hope you'll know that you are more, and that there's so much more in store (for you, of course)!

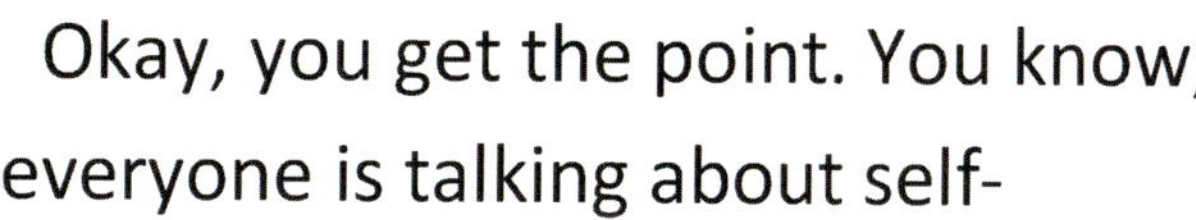

Okay, you get the point. You know, everyone is talking about self-discovery and valuing yourself and being true to yourself, but whoever thought to ask, who are YOU? Perhaps you have. I think we all do.

You all know about the cosmic big bang. You know, not the one you make at the party, but that big bang when life all started. Did it ever start? How could something begin from nothing? I think it always was. At least, spiritually.

 And whether you call this "always-ness" God or Creator or whatever name you like, it's still the same. It WAS in the beginning. It IS in the NOW and it will BE in the ending. Of course, it's all in the eternal Now. Make sense or not yet? The cool thing is, we are part of this divinity, part of this incredible universe in a very real way.

I think when growing up there is this tendency to feel separated from life, from others. You know, you start separating out from your parents. You want to know, why am I here? What's the deal? And this is okay. It's good, even. You've got to ask questions if you'd like to find answers.

Some people rebel against their parents. Mostly, they find out later their parents were right. But, we come from our parents, or did we? Well, we should respect them because, after all, they work hard for us. They sweat, they stress, they worry. Actually, none of these are necessary, but they do it anyhow. The point is, they give their life for us. Hey, just wait till you get there, then you'll believe me!

So, here we are in this little body and nobody listens to us because they think we don't know anything! They don't even know that we are ancient souls and it doesn't matter what the age of our body is. The wisdom is deep inside of you. There's more on reincarnation, but we'll talk about that one later.

So, who here likes gardening? If you haven't done it yet, try it! It's really amazing to see what comes up when you put a little seed in the ground. It looks dead by all outer appearances, but, wow, when it grows, it just awes me. It's ALIVE! What intelligence! Who put it there? I think you know the answer to that.

So, back to seeds. You're a divine seed. Yep. Absolutely. I'm not sure what variety – that's up to you to decide. But the gardener, who could that be? Yep, God. And even more cool, the whole product is God.

So, you're a God-seed right now. And we're all growing into our God-hood!

You know, you may be thinking, isn't that blasphemy? That's what Jesus said and they thought he was insulting God saying he was the Son of God (which we are too, by the way). But, God-hood? What does that even mean? What it doesn't mean is everyone bowing to you and only you. But did you know that the angels bow to you? Yeah, they bow to the light in your heart. That's God right there and they serve and worship God. What God-hood doesn't mean is changing the rules of the universe. Not yet, anyhow! But think about it. Kids grow up to be adults like their parents. If we are children of God, which we are, then what are we destined for? To grow up to be divinely magnificent like our Father-Mother God.

Now, actually, here's a secret. You already ARE magnificent! It's all you really are already. You just didn't know it…but now you do!

In a spiritual nutshell:

All you've got to remember is, your beginning was cosmically awesome and you come from a divine seed – God! Self-discovery doesn't get any cooler than that!

Unscramble the letters to see what you've known all along!

UYO REA MAED FO DOG TUSFF!

____

CH 2: So, Why am I Here? What do I do With My Life?

Do you know why you're here? Aside from being born to your parents, that is! Well, spiritually speaking, we actually all have a mission. A mission that is possible! And not only possible, but planned. Who planned it for you? You did! Are you surprised?

Before this life, we planned with our guardian spirits and angels what we would

do and experience this time around. So there we were, standing there, reviewing our life and making plans and now here we are, on the other side! The other side of the screen of life and we've totally forgotten it all. Do you believe it?

But I can't remember any of it, you say. Ah, but that is part of the test! Would it be so

hard if you could see and remember everything always? Life doesn't always have cheat sheets. But it does have reminders. Consider this one of them.

So, okay. What now? Say this is true, what does this mean for my life? Well, it certainly means you weren't an accident and that everything happens for a reason.

Even your less enjoyable experiences can help you learn lessons. About yourself, and others. Anyhow, so much for the past. Let's look to the future.

This is your time to shine! Your chance to be a hero! Fortunately, it's actually really easy. Just be true to yourself. That's it! But first you've got to know yourself (see the first chapter). How can you be true to yourself if you don't even know who you are...and I'm not talking about your name and address here. It's much deeper than that.

When we all are true to ourselves, this world will be transformed. In fact, it IS being transformed right now by people all over the globe who are being true to their inner mission. Watch their joy, hope, miracles, music, inspiration and new technologies come forth! And don't just watch it, get in on the act!

A lot of people, especially when they're young, want to be famous. It doesn't matter if your heavenly contract, your divine plan, is glamourous and well-known or simple and humble. What matters is that it's *yours.*

Have you ever tasted that feeling of just being so alive because you're doing something that you love? Like, you don't want to stop what you're doing to eat or sleep because it just makes you feel good and it's 'you'? If you've never felt that feeling, look at what you're good at. Ask family and friends. Pray about it. If you think about what you are good at, what skills you have and what others appreciate in you, these can all give you clues as to where your destiny lies.

There's a saying, "Better your own dharma (i.e. mission), fulfilled imperfectly, then someone else's done perfectly." You see, you can't throw down the bat and walk away. Your mission is your mission and if you don't do it, who will? Am I sounding dramatic? Sorry. But it's true.

At a spiritual level, we each hold a balance. Known or unknown, we do it.

What I am so excited about is that we are entering this new age with so many advanced souls (including you!). Would you even have found this path if it were not for your past attainment and the promises you made to God to find it again in this life? I think not.

So, my friends, channel your own divinity. Do you know what a channel is? It's something through which something else can flow. So, you're the channel, and you channel God. Sounds pretty cool, huh? You do it all the time, but are just not aware of it, maybe. God is always streaming his/her energy/light/consciousness into you, sustaining you, loving you, blessing you and giving you ideas and even life itself.

Are you receptive? Are you open? Can you find what you love and draw down something, some idea, some inspiration, something from God every day to transform that skill or talent that you will one day deliver to the world in a very real way? As your mission is developed and given to bless this earth, the

world will be a brighter place because you live in
it.

Piano anyone?

There's a girl named Emily Bear who plays the piano and writes her own music. She's just 6 years old. At least, she was at the time when she said, "This comes out to me, this comes out." These were her words as she played a beautiful piece on the piano. When the interviewer asked her, "Where does it come from?" she just smiled sweetly and said, "I don't know… probably my heart," as she shrugged towards heaven. Now, that's the way to work! Today, at 13 she continues to compose and perform and even has orchestras performing her music with her![1]

Young people of the new age, this is your age, this is your time to shine! Thank you for sharing your gifts!

---

[1] "Emily Bear: Girl With A Gift. A WGN News Special," Published on July 25, 2013, https://youtu.be/HhjzNG0wSGY.

ACTIVITY: Treasure Mapping!

Who likes treasure? Everyone! In this activity, you all get to have the treasure! But first you have to make a treasure map!

A treasure map is a fun type of project which is kind of like scrapbooking what you want in life. You get pictures and words out of catalogues and magazines (or wherever) and paste them all together. This represents your goals. Choose images and words that show what you'd like to accomplish in the next two or three years.

What are some goals you have? Perhaps you'd like to learn to swim, ride a horse, learn a musical instrument, take up martial arts, learn another language or become a good cook.

Maybe you'd like to practice public speaking or painting or rock climbing. If computer programming or babysitting is on your list, put that down

too. Perhaps you'd like to volunteer in a way that helps others and makes them smile.

Whatever it is, think about it, then put it on your treasure map. Then talk to your parents and God about it and see what goals you can

manifest in your life. It is exciting as you realize that you can set goals and that you can accomplish them. If you can do that with a small thing, what can you do with your whole life ahead of you?

Treasure Map

Finding your Mission is truly a-Maze-ing!

CH 3: Your actions matter – Here's why, and what to do about it!

Farmers just get it. They understand it. When you plant a bean seed, you get a bean. When you plant a corn seed you get corn. What you plant (or sow), you harvest (or reap). And

that's what Jesus said. Not that you'd doubt him if you were a farmer. You'd already know it.

As you sow, so shall you reap.

It actually applies to your life, not just the dirt in your backyard!

Have you heard the proverb, "What goes around comes around?" "Cause and effect" is the scientific way to put it. It basically means something happened that caused an effect. Pretty basic, I know.

Quiz Time!

Jesus also said, you shall know every man by their:
a) Fruits
b) Bread
c) Drinks
d) All of the above

It's even in religion. Some religions that believe your actions in this life affect your next life are Hinduism, Buddhism, Sikhism and Christianity, although in the last case, they don't believe you could have another life on earth.[2]

It's a good thing a lot of people believe their actions matter because it helps society be 'good'. Jesus was the most famous one to state the Golden Rule, but did you know that many others have stated it too? Here are some examples. It's everywhere – you'd think it was like a universal rule or something!

Bahá'í Faith: *Ascribe not to any soul that which thou wouldst not have ascribed to thee, and say not that which thou doest not.*
  Baha'u'llah

Christianity: *All things whatsoever ye would that men should do to you, do ye so to them; for this is the law and the prophets.*
  Matthew 7:1

Confucianism: *Do not do to others what you would not like yourself.*
  Analects 12:2

---

[2] That's mainstream Christianity. The less known followers of Jesus have always believed in it.

Buddhism: *Hurt not others in ways that you yourself would find hurtful.*
Udana-Varga 5,1

Hinduism: *This is the sum of duty; do naught unto others what you would not have them do unto you.*
Mahabharata 5,1517

Islam: *No one of you is a believer until he desires for his brother that which he desires for himself.*
Sunnah

Jainism: *A man should wander about treating all creatures as he himself would be treated.*
Sutrakritanga 1.11.33

Judaism: *What is hateful to you, do not do to your fellowman. This is the entire Law; all the rest is commentary.*
Talmud, Shabbat 3id

Native American Spirituality: *All things are our relatives; what we do to everything, we do to ourselves. All is really One.*
Black Elk

Taoism: *Regard your neighbor's gain as your gain, and your neighbor's loss as your own loss.*
Tai Shang Kan Yin P'ien

Zoroastrianism: *That nature alone is good which refrains from doing another whatsoever is not good for itself.*
Dadisten-I-dinik, 94,5

Wow, what a lot! And some pretty complicated words for some of you. It just all basically says the same thing, which is that you should treat others the way you would like to be treated. Because, sooner or later it WILL come back to you!

So, why do we get everything back to us? I think it's partly because it's God's law and he wants to teach us what is good, how to be good. And partly it's because we are connected so we really are doing it to ourselves. Because we really are all in this giant spider web together (well, not quite, but we are connected), we really are hurting/helping ourselves in the grand, ultimate scheme of things.

Okay, you've probably got the point by now, right? Well, almost. Every day we do things – in our actions, words and even thoughts. This is something we all do. Can we make all of those pure and loving and harmonious? We can start with the most important things, our actions, and work backwards, changing our words and then our thoughts. Then again, sometimes it's easier to just start by changing your thoughts!

Whatever you do, make it sweet, because you'll get to taste it again!

Jesus once said…

Keeping these words in mind, what have you done to Jesus in your life so far and what areas could you improve on?

____

____

____

____

____

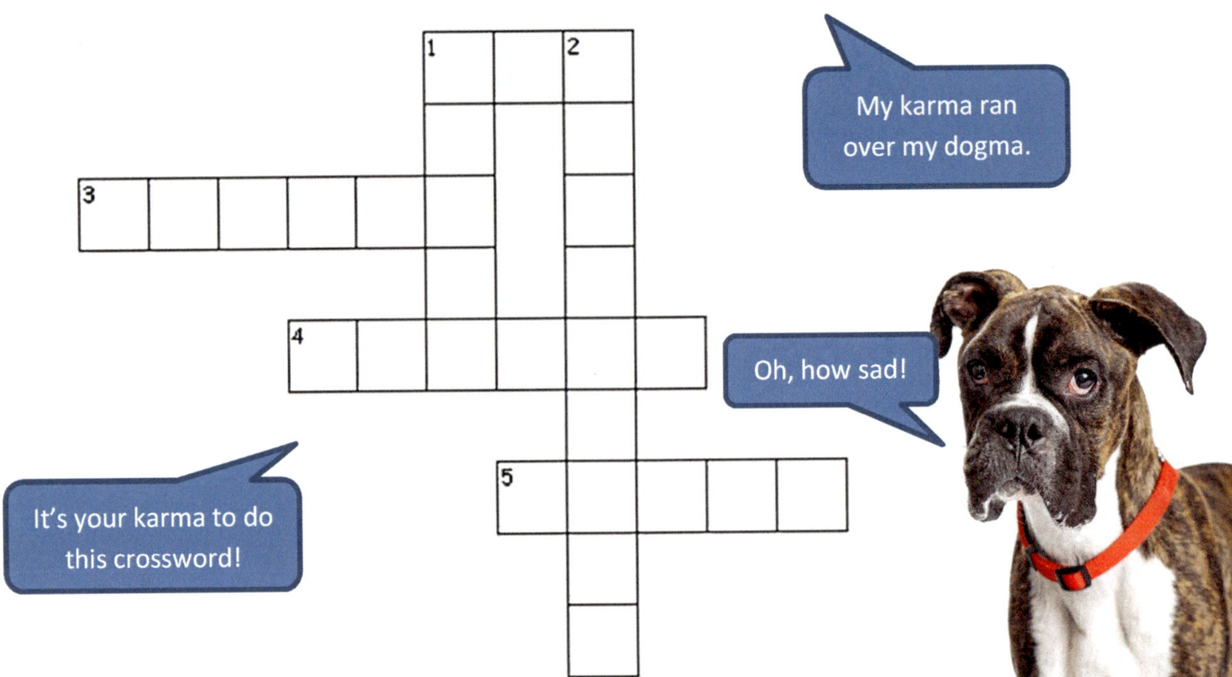

Across
1. what a spider makes and what spiritually connects us
3. what we have every day when we decide how to act
4. the best rule to follow
5. the stuff that comes back to you
Down
1. a symbol of karma, it goes around and around
2. fun to throw, a great example of karma from the Australian continent

CH 4: Been there, done that!

"All the world's a stage, and all the men and women merely players. They have their exits and their entrances."
— William Shakespeare

Have you ever had the feeling that you've done something before? Well, you just may have! It's an ancient idea. You could say it's 'been around'. And keeps coming back! It's reincarnation. What's that all about? Pretty simple really. We're spirits, not just these physical bodies we wear. And we require more time to fulfill our purpose and learn our lessons well. So, God gives us another chance. And another. There's nothing quite like a second chance. Except, well, a second chance.

When you look to nature for confirmation of this, you see cycles of life and death, of new birth and rebirth everywhere you look. Each fall the trees 'die' to all outer appearances as their leaves fall to the ground. The bulbs die back each season leaving no trace. The seeds lie inactive in the ground waiting for the right conditions to fulfill their purpose. And, speaking of the seasons, they themselves are cycles. And so is night and day. What is sleep but a mini 'end' of life, only to begin the next day continuing your memory of the previous day, unlike a past life. The universe is full of cycles and we are a part of that universe. Thank you God for cycles of opportunity and cycles of rest, and for the chance to try again!

So, what could you do with this kind of information about the existence of past lives? How could it help you or change your perspective on life if you knew you'd lived before? Well, for one thing, you probably deserve what you've got! The situations you find yourself in now were actually created by past life choices, right down to the wonderful parents or the challenging siblings. Or anything else for that matter.

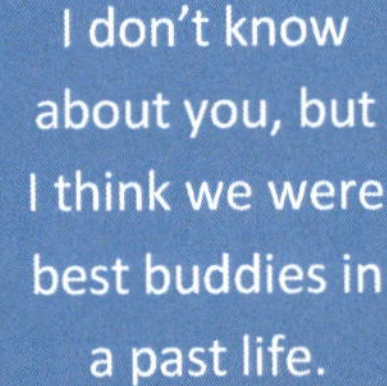

Do you think it's your parent's fault that they have a bad habit or attitude that you couldn't help but be exposed to? Or that you had passed on to you that physical imperfection or genetic weakness? Well, you know what? You actually chose your parents and they chose you! In the spirit world, that is. And the things that you don't like about them, you actually have inside you from past lives and that's why you were drawn to your parents. So that you could resolve it, take responsibility for it or come to peace with it once and for all.

Wow, I don't recognize myself. Did I die and come back?

Is this idea hard to swallow? Maybe. Maybe not. Depends on what your life is like at this point in time! I know it's easier to blame others sometimes. But in the long run, freedom comes from being free, from being responsible and accountable and saying, God, you are fair and just and I'll work with what is mine that you gave back to me to resolve, even if I don't remember my past lives.

And speaking of that, have you ever wondered if we have past lives, why on earth can't we remember them? It would just be too complicated, that's why! Can you imagine just

Some people actually have memories of past lives. If you do, that's okay. If you don't, that's okay too. God only gives us what we are ready to deal with.

how many different relationships we've had with so many different people and how it's way simpler and easier to just learn the lessons one by one that God gives us, with the people in our life today?

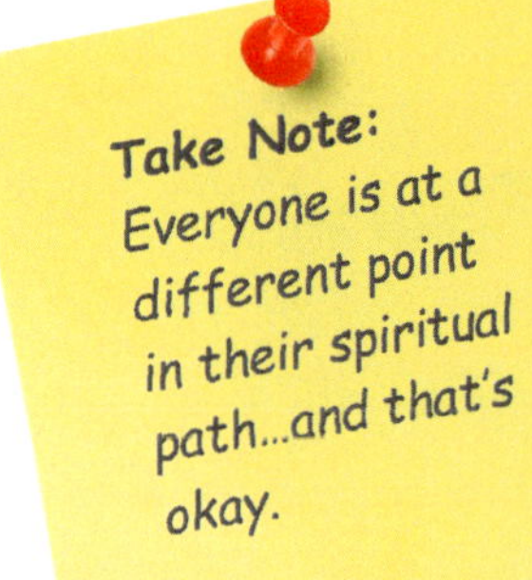

Have you ever seen a child prodigy on TV? You know, those kids that become famous because they are still kids but they have some incredible musical, artistic or mathematical talent that is way beyond most adults? Where do you think they got that talent? Past lives! I know, I know, some of them have spent hours practicing it since they were three. But others, it's a talent beyond comprehension. It's a gift from the start.

God is fair, right? I think so. So, what gives? Why is there so much disparity on the earth and so much difference between people and what they have or do not have? I think past lives help us answer that, because who knows what we or others have done in their past to get where they are today.

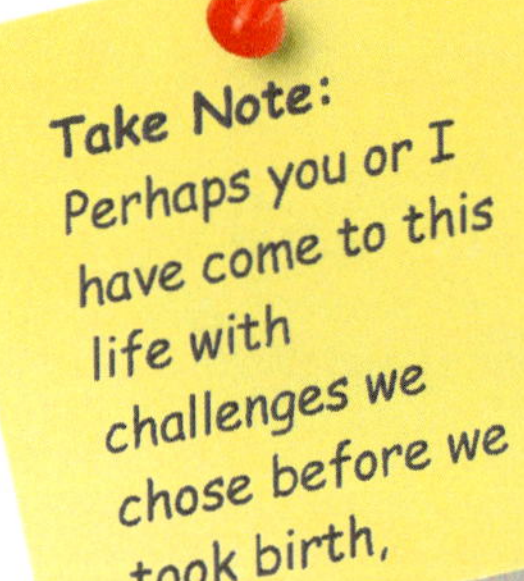

Now, does this mean that you look down on the homeless dude or the poor African child because it's their karma from a past life? Not at all! It could be you, after all, if it wasn't for God's grace. We can choose the higher way of trying to help those around us, while also realizing that karma is a player.

There's another player too. It's the lesson. Can you believe that some great, advanced souls, choose to come to earth solely to teach us lessons and that they sometimes choose to come back in a body or situation that seems bad? Perhaps it is to simply remind us that God lives in all!

Let me give you an example of this. Mattie Stepanek was born with a sad medical condition and yet his heart was so advanced. I think he was way beyond most of us! He died at 13. But what a life! What a message!

His books became bestsellers and he was interviewed on TV. But that's not the important bit. He started writing these messages and poems as young as 3 years old. He called them Heartsongs because, "It was the song in my heart. It was the message in my heart." It was all about being a peacemaker.

This sweet little boy who was confined to a wheelchair said, "I really think I'm here for a purpose because in my life I have had so many close calls to dying, even if it takes me one year or one thousand years, I have to do what I was meant to do."[3] God bless that little Mattie, that great soul. Check him out on YouTube. It will make you cry. And you'll know what I mean about being an advanced soul.

And, speaking of souls, that's what we are. We're not this body we call ourselves. It's a jacket, it's a car, a vehicle, even a pet. When we come into this life we 'die' in the other world and are 'born' into this world. Our soul and spirit enters our

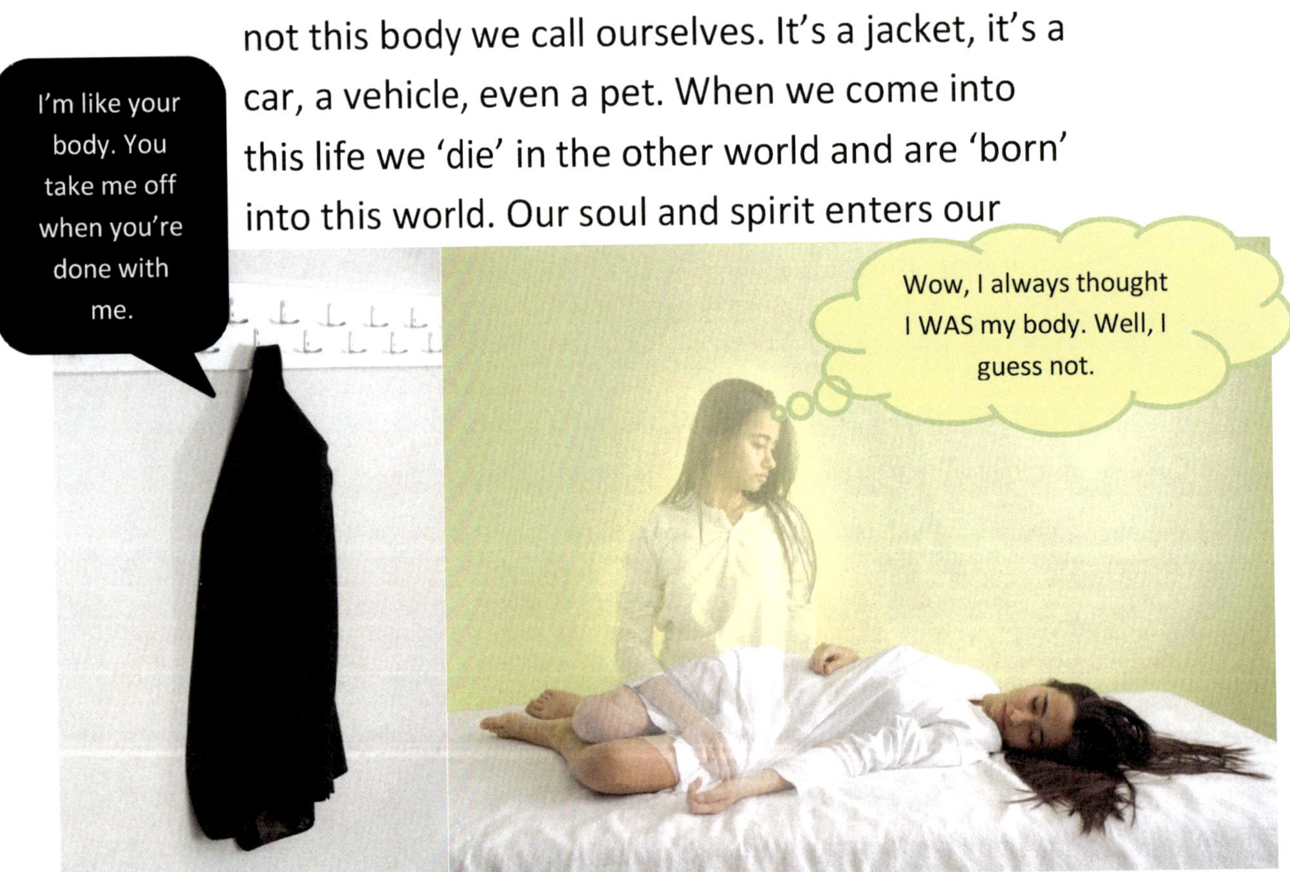

---

[3] "Oprah 20th Anniversary Heartprints Mattie.avi," Published on October 17, 2012, https://youtu.be/B2Rg9TTuoDE.

26

body and becomes one with it and unable, mostly, to leave it again.

After some while of babyhood we start to associate with this cute new body that we've woken up into and are getting better at controlling day by day. We can now get the spoon of baby cereal into our mouth – yay! As distractions happen and we become more and more involved in worldly life most of us forget the realms we came from. But we're not just a body that dies of old age one day. We're a spirit of God that can enter a body and have different experiences. Many experiences!

You know, you're more ancient than you think! So, next time you think, been there, done that, yep, you probably have!

WHAT DID THE BOY SAY TO THE OLD MAN?

A	B	C	D	E	F	G	H	I	J	K	L	M	N	O	P	Q	R	S	T	U	V	W	X	Y	Z
3				19			7						2							21					

"I _ I _ _ _ ' _ _ _ E _ I E _ E _ I _
7 5 7 5 13 18 14 19 9 7 19 25 19 7 13

_ E I _ _ A _ _ A _ I O _ _ A _ _ _ O U _
23 19 7 13 15 3 23 13 3 18 7 2 13 3 18 16 2 21 23

A _ E _ E I _ _ E _ . "
3 22 19 19 7 18 24 19 23

CH 5: You are a Powerful Spiritual Being

You are a powerful spiritual being. Yes, I'll say it again, you are a powerful spiritual being! Why do you not feel it some days? It is karma and the life we live here. It can be a bit dense at times. And besides, that's part of the test. It would be easy if we remembered it always. What I'd like you to know is that you are all powerful beings for good in the universe. You have unlimited energy at your command. Does this sound a bit sci-fi to you? Well, it is. It's cosmic! Only it's real! And then again, truth is stranger than fiction. That's how the saying goes. And it's true. It often is.

So, what does one do with one's newfound power? How does one wield it? Well, for good and truth in the kingdom!

Actually, in many ways. Did you know, for example, that we are all healers? We can heal in many ways. It's not we that heals, of course, but God. But then again, it's the same thing. Just don't get all arrogant about it. It's God doing the work. We can heal others with our words, our words of kindness and honesty and appreciation and acceptance. We can heal with our tone of voice – caring, strong, reassuring and encouraging.

We can heal with our hands. Did you know that you have sacred energy centers in your hands that actually emit or give off a spiritual radiance? I wouldn't be surprised if they also gave off an electrical charge too. It's not just Jesus and his mother Mary who can have their hands stream forth light like the artwork shows. We're all supposed to do it. Hands have been used for healing in the Christian tradition of laying on of hands.

You can even heal with your eyes. You can send light rays through your eyes. Everyone looks at the eyes because they truly are the windows to the soul. You feel someone's spirit by looking into their eyes. Just like you can take in things with your eyes, you can shine light out through them! Just ask God to do this and he/she will. As you practice seeing God in yourself and others you use your eyes in the way God intended. And what you do well gets multiplied and made more powerful!

How else can you help the world in a spiritual way with just what you have today? Well, you can imagine a better world. You can visualize (which means have a visual in front of your eyes!). You can put feeling into your imagination. You can set your intent before heaven that you choose to be a light worker, a person who they can use for good and to please show you how to do just that. Before long you'll be changing the world for good. And that's a good thing, because the world could do with a bit of change!

Let's Imagine!

What would the perfect world look like to you? What would you do if you had unlimited power to work good in the world?

____

____

____

____

____

____

PS. You _do_ have unlimited power in God!

CH 6: Heaven Has Powerful Spiritual beings too!

Just as you are a powerful spiritual being, there are powerful spiritual beings in the heaven world too! Only they are even more powerful! And of course, they're in heaven. But they're also on earth too, through our prayers!

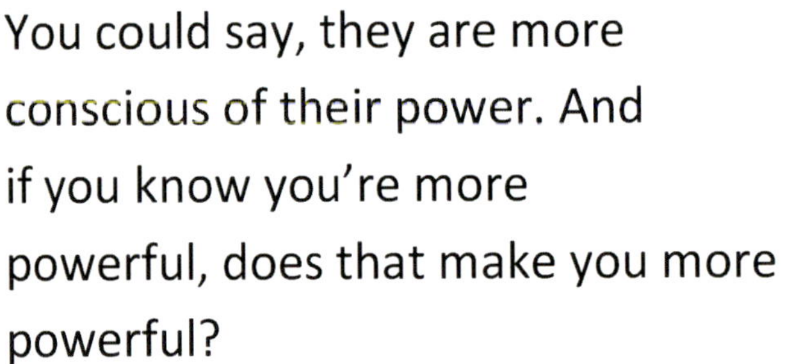

You could say, they are more conscious of their power. And if you know you're more powerful, does that make you more powerful?

Probably. They also have a lot more Self-realization and experience, a lot more passed tests and attainment. In any case, you can be great buddies with these awesome spiritual dudes. And one day you can be one of them. Just think of them as your very own personal superheroes

and archetypes. The real type. The spiritual type. Very cool!

To think of them a different way, just imagine for a moment that you have a magic lamp and that all you have to do is rub that lamp and a genie will come out and grant your wishes. Ta dah! How awesome! (Assuming you ask for wise things, of course. No stupid wishes!)

Well now, you do have a genie! God, through all of the angels, is your cosmic genie. The angels will do whatever you ask them, as long as it is in accordance with God's will. If you ask for goodness, for goodwill, for kindness, for blessing, for the betterment of your family and nation, for showers of blessings, for the protection of freedom everywhere and on and on, they will do it! You just have to ask. That's it.

Sometimes they can't change a situation if someone has a lesson to learn. In other situations, they perform the kinds of miracles or 'coincidences' you sometimes hear about in news stories and read about in *Chicken Soup for the Soul* books. There really *are* miracles in this world...And the angels really are pretty busy! It's a good thing there are lots of them to go around...and that time and space mean nothing to them! Actually, they like having a job, so set them to work in your world today!

You might be asking, well, how are guides aka saints aka Ascended Masters different from angels? Well, they're just a different type of God-being. They all work for God so call to whichever you feel closest to. If you come from a Christian background, then you'll likely feel closer to Jesus.

If you grew up Catholic, you'll likely be familiar

with the Virgin Mary or Saint Michael the Archangel. If you've come from a Buddhist background then maybe Buddha or Kuan Yin is your best bet. If you have a Hindu background, then maybe Lakshmi or Shiva or Krishna is your best friend.

And it doesn't really matter. It's all God. And it's all good!

Feeling adventurous? There are so many cool masters and beings of light in the other worlds. There are more than there are stars, or at least, stars you can count. And that's a lot! There are masters that we have heard the names of in Greek and Roman mythology who are actually real beings. How about Hercules? Athena anyone? Venus or Vesta? God Mercury?

Then you've got modern saints so throw in Mother Teresa, Ramakrishna, Omraam and many others and you've got quite a mix. A good mix. Don't worry, they all get along!

It might seem strange but in some ways it's actually more normal than the other way of thinking. Everything, or at least, true religion, all has bits of truth in it. Your task is to follow that thread back to the sun of your own divinity where your own Higher Self wears a silken garment of gold. And don't worry, you won't unravel it by following the thread!

The angels, the buddhas, and there are many of them, the Catholic saints (not that one church can 'own' a saint!) and all of the Hindu deities. These are just some of the many divine beings in heaven. And hopefully, we'll add your name to the list one day!

Search For the Divine Ones!

```
H O O C X P O Z L H R J N R T N M D P W J
D K N T K M V R Z V E J E S U S E A U M A
Y I H O E N M A I T R E Y A I E L U S N B
Y G V G R N I M J R M Q P R Q L C Y H U H
Q S A I N T P A T R I C K A A U H S E C J
C K G T N Q A A M H A R B S D C I C O E N
O M O T H E R T E R E S A V G R Z N R N P
N O D B N I D S E I E T A A K E E Q M N S
F T F B Y I A I X M H G H T M H D P F H W
U H R L I L R T R E H C T I T M E E I F Q
C E E N P K T P N E T L C N A V K V U O S
I R U H S N S A K E C H F E I M A A R M O
U M A H D D U B A M A T U A G A B R I E L
S A I N T T H E R E S E O F L I S I E U X
A R G P P G T H L K C G C R L N A O L G A
E Y A S A N A T K U M A R A P O C I T P W
V I R P T Z R N H U Z R K I Z Z B W S W G
N A H O H C A H A M R S E K U A N Y I N B
G H Y J M A Z O U I H V W C I M U H T U K
B N N B V L E J M M C H I R U A O X A X J
K C F Z J I E L I K U T W Y E W W X I L I
```

KUAN YIN	GABRIEL	BRAHMA	VAJRASATTVA
MAITREYA	RAPHAEL	EL MORYA	SARASVATI
MOTHER MARY	CONFUCIUS	DIVINE DIRECTOR	JOHN THE BAPTIST
JESUS	CUZCO	AFRA	METATRON
GAUTAMA BUDDHA	ENOCH	KUTHUMI	MAHA CHOHAN
PADRE PIO	HERCULES	SANAT KUMARA	OMRAAM
MOTHER TERESA	AMAZONIA	GODFRE	
SHIVA	MELCHIZEDEK	PALLAS ATHENA	
KRISHNA	ALPHA	SAINT THERESE OF LISIEUX	
LAKSHMI	OMEGA	SAINT PATRICK	
ZARATHUSTRA	SAINT GERMAIN		
MICHAEL	URIEL		

CH 7: So you'd like to become an Ascended Master?

Hey, let me shake your hand dude! Congratulations on one of the best choices you've ever made in your life...or was that lifetimes? I knew you had it in you!

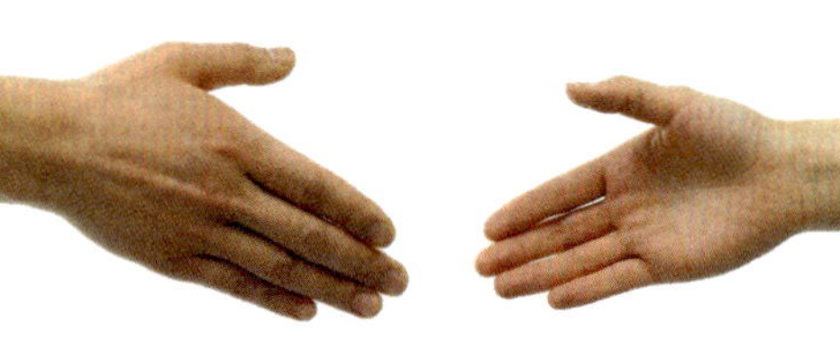

"Er, ah, what?" you say. Well, you know what you just decided, right? "Uh, yeah, I think so." You go buddy! The decision to become an Ascended Master is a life-altering one. Take a seat while I talk you through this one.

You reach behind you and find conveniently, a soft, comfortable armchair. Sinking into its softness you relax and begin thinking about your choice.

Yeah, it was a big one, you think. Then again, maybe not.

After all, for the longest time, people have dreamed of a heavenly afterworld in which to spend their existence. Whether it was the Native American "happy hunting ground," the Australian Aboriginal Dreamtime, the Buddhist Nirvana or the Christian heaven. Or any other variation. Did you know that almost all of the world believes in *some* form of afterlife? At least, they used to. And almost all native peoples do. Even the ancient Greeks did. The belief is everywhere. Well, anyhow, you're okay with the idea.

Not that you can change it by believing in it or not. It either is or it isn't. You'll have to wait till you die to find out! But, seriously, is there something you can do in this

life that will affect how you are in the next? You shift uncomfortably in your chair, deep in thought.

"How can one choice made now, affect the future of my life forever?" The answers begin to flow into your mind. Well, in one sense, it doesn't matter, you can always make a new choice if you don't like the way your life is going. On the other hand, you won't be in this body forever so it's a good time to make lasting choices now.

So what do you want to believe and how do you get there?

Now some believe in reincarnation but do you really want to do that forever? It's good when you need it, but not forever! After all, who really wants to come back in diapers again and again and again only to grow old and die. Forever. There's got to be a better way.

Scratching your chin, you think about the two afterlives you know most about. Buddhist nirvana or Christian heaven. They both sound pretty good to you. One is bliss forever; the other a heavenly garden forever, or thereabouts.

But this, this is a new idea. It wasn't till today that you'd heard the idea of becoming an Ascended Master. Apparently it's like Buddhist Nirvana crossed with Christian heaven with a few extras thrown in! You would be okay with that. After all, you could handle prancing across the galaxies to some far off galactic star. Or spending time learning higher technology with masters of divine science. Heaven is not the end of it all – just the beginning!

Alrighty, you think, settling upon the idea. It has been a good choice. But what next? How to get there? You need a roadmap, but where? Involuntarily you reach down, into your pocket and pull out a map. Cool! Things are going well for you today! As you unfold it, you realize this is no ordinary map. It's personalized just for you and it's a map showing you the path to take to become an Ascended Master!

As your eyes focus in on the details you notice that there are many Ys in your life, many places in your life where you will have to make a choice. You notice, that, while some choices don't matter so much, others will take you away from your path or lead you further ahead. Those are the ones you want to pay attention to!

After reading the map over you notice a note down at the bottom. Apparently, it's a little more complicated. To become an Ascended Master, you have to master yourself – thoughts, feelings, words, deeds and 'ascend' – merge with God – or maybe, realize you already *are* part of God! And you also have to do this little thing called balance your karma, aka payback time! Another reason to make lots of good karma and not so much bad karma. Then there's the little issue of your divine plan. You came to do it and you've got to do it. There's no way around it if you want to ascend. Fortunately, it's the thing your soul loves to do and is good at so that's not an issue.

Wow, so much to remember. Fortunately, you have this little map to remind you of the way. You fold it up neatly and stick it back carefully in your pants pocket.

Yawning, you stand up. That's enough reading and seriousness for today. And that's when you hear your mom calling, "Hey, wake up sleepyhead, you've got 10 minutes left for breakfast!"

Can You Find Your Way In?

44

CH 8: Tests are coming – and I don't mean school tests!

There is a time in your life when you will be tested. Not the school spelling tests; no, much more important. Life tests. Ewww! Does that make you lean back in your seat? Who likes tests anyhow?

Tests can be a good thing or a bad thing. It depends how you look at it. You can learn a lot as you prepare for a test. And you can learn from the test, from what you got wrong. You can even learn how much there still is to know!

And you know, that's like our whole life, really. There are always challenges with our karma or even God testing us. Did you know that God likes to test us? Yeah, that can be a strange idea. God doesn't do it to make us fail. I think he/she wants us to pass our tests and go to the next grade, to the next schoolroom called the heaven worlds. Ha! That's graduation all right.

So, there's this spiritual teaching that your karma from past lives starts returning at age 12. So that gives you up till then to get your spiritual life in order.

Childhood is a great time to prepare for your future – while living in the NOW!

As you move through life you may face peer pressure. Haven't felt it yet? You're fortunate! Peer pressure is when everyone else around you – your peers – subtly or not so subtly think you should do things differently and you feel that pressure to conform. What will you do? Your mom's probably already given you the, "what if everyone else jumps off a cliff?" line.

It takes a strong person to sail from childhood to adulthood while being true to yourself. Often you look for friends all around you. The best friend you can ever find is God and others that respect you for being true to that God. You know, the best, most satisfying relationships come from being around those who respect you and value you for being yourself.

When you're true to yourself, you'll know it, and everyone else will too. You'll just have that extra something that no one can quite pin down.

And when you take the lead by being a leader and not a follower, you'll be an example and sooner or later others will follow you.

We all desire love, respect and appreciation. And we all deserve it too! The thing is, make sure you're getting it from the right source. You can't compromise yourself in the process.

Whatever relationships you get into growing up, whether friendships or more, make sure that you are with a friend of like heart, a friend who lifts you up or

at least supports you spiritually. A true friend desires the best for us. A true friend never pressures. If it isn't a true friendship, it's not worth having.

The world we live in today can challenge your morals at times, or your faith in God. It's not the easiest place to live if you are on a different road at times or walking the opposite direction from the crowd. But, then again, who wants to be like a sheep, following the flock over the cliff. You know, they really do that? They really do walk straight over the cliff simply because the sheep in front of them did. Wow! Thank God we aren't sheep. At least we have free will, conscious awareness and choice.

Now, in future golden ages upon Earth, it will be easy to follow the crowd – because we'll all be going the right way! Going with the flow will be right *and* easy!

In the meantime, just reassure yourself. We are the way showers and the truth speakers. We are the forerunners of this New Day. And God made us strong enough to survive and to thrive and do what we have to do to be happy, to be loved and most importantly, to be true to our Self.

> *"This above all: to thine own self be true"*
>
> – William Shakespeare, *Hamlet*

Q. What does being true to You mean?

____

____

____

CH 9: Got Connection?

One of the most important things that we can do to help us be true to our Self, is to connect with that Self!

This funny picture illustrates this idea. Of course, it's not quite accurate. The wisdom actually comes from within, not above. So maybe the next picture is actually more accurate.

Of course, God can be above as well as within. God is everywhere - duh!

And spiritually speaking, the God Presence is above you (in vibration), but it's also right in your heart. Jesus said, the kingdom of God is within you.

And, while we're talking about Jesus, here's a cool story if I ever heard one! Check out this girl's connection with Jesus:

A sweet little girl named Megan had a great love for Jesus. She was only 5 years old when she heard someone talk about dating Jesus but she liked the idea anyhow. She took it very seriously, getting her room prepared as well as preparing herself, before sitting down at her toy table in full faith, to wait for Jesus.

She says, "And that is when I heard a knock on the door." Wow. Yes, Jesus walked right into her room! He sat down and smiled at her and they had 'tea' together, talking about whatever she felt like discussing. When her 'tea' date was over, Jesus then invited her on a journey of his own. He took her in a heavenly carriage pulled by two white horses. As they went, Jesus described many places

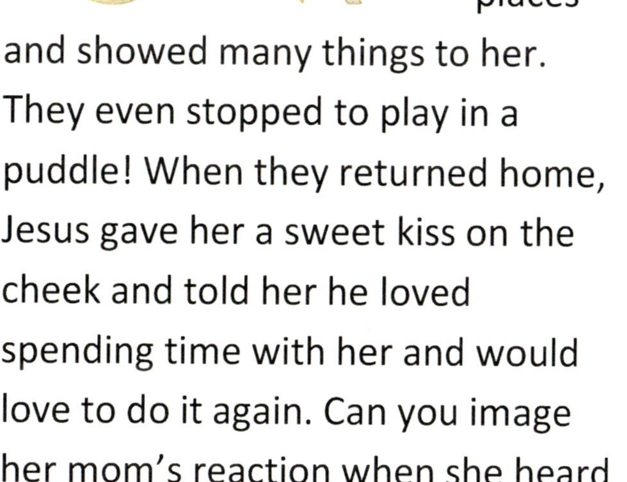

and showed many things to her. They even stopped to play in a puddle! When they returned home, Jesus gave her a sweet kiss on the cheek and told her he loved spending time with her and would love to do it again. Can you image her mom's reaction when she heard about it!

This was the beginning – and what a beginning – of a close relationship with Jesus. Megan is now 13 years old and has had many special experiences, from drinking from a bubbling cup of joy, to dancing with Jesus, to visiting heavenly gardens with him. Way too much detail to retell right here! But please check out the book yourself if you're interested.[4]

Megan is not so concerned about the amazing things going on in her life or what she can get out of Jesus. She just truly loves being with him, and by God's grace this – and her faith – opened doors for her, literally. Hey, even if they were spiritual doors!

For anyone doubting her story, she has changed in the eyes of her family. She has become

spiritually wise with the stuff Jesus shares with her, and even her brother is now having spiritual visits to heaven![5]

Now, that girl has connection! Love, faith and a pure motive worked for her. It will work for you too!

---

[4] Toldeo, Jennifer, *Children and the Supernatural* (Florida: Charisma House, 2012), 53-68. The book is actually written for adults but this story is worth reading by everyone!

[5] Toldeo, Jennifer, *Children and the Supernatural.* Thanks to the author for capturing this precious and incredible story in detail!

Another well-known way to connect with God is prayer. All religions, or at least all the ones I can think of, use prayer of some sort. A prayer is a verbal connection to Spirit, invoking, thanking, asking, affirming, praising and more. You can do a lot of things with prayer!

Here's something good to remember. If you're ever having a rough day at home or school, there are legions of angels always available and literally waiting for you to call to them 24/7. They love to help you with anything and everything! If ever you or someone you know feels down and out, call to Archeia Hope (Archeia is the female equivalent of Archangel). If you're lacking faith, try Archeia Faith! How about a need for

charity? There's Archeia Charity! Faith, Hope and Charity! Whoever knew they could be mighty beings and not just qualities!

They can answer your questions too!

How to find the answer…. a story

Once upon a time, there was a child who yearned to know the mysteries of life.

And so he would ask his parents many questions. And when they would answer, he would then often say, "Why?" And they would do their best to communicate the reasons for the answers that they gave, but at a certain point they could no longer share fully the knowledge that he sought. And so they recommended to him that he simply ask his heart the answer to the "Why?"

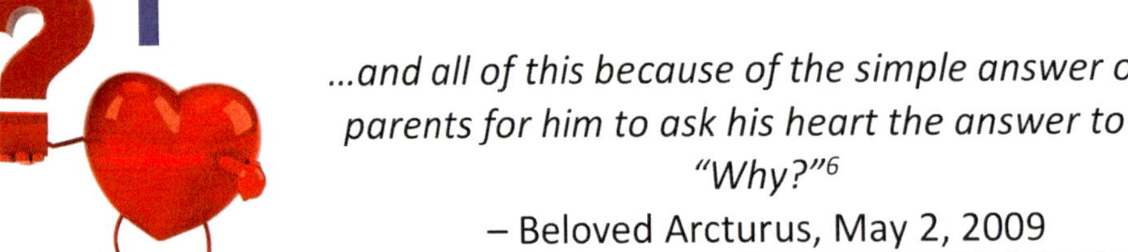

And this little boy did. And you would be amazed at what he discovered when he performed this very simple ritual after his parents could no longer fulfill his need to answer every question. And so he would sit in silence and ponder the answer within his heart. And then later his parents would ask him what he discovered, and he would share with them the deepest mysteries of life that his heart conveyed unto his mind. And they were amazed at the inner knowledge that this little one received in communion with his heart.

This went on for a number of months.
And though at a certain point the boy stopped asking his parents the question "Why?" but still continued to ask his heart the answers to his inner questions, he continued to grow in divine wisdom and understanding.

…and all of this because of the simple answer of his parents for him to ask his heart the answer to the "Why?"[6]
– Beloved Arcturus, May 2, 2009

---

[6] Lewis, David Christopher. "A Bedtime Story from Our Godparents, the Elohim" by Arcturus. The Hearts Center. http://www.heartscenter.org/TeachingsBlogs/ HeartStreamsandDiscourses/TheHeartStreamsDatabase/tabid/66/afn/090502- Arcturus-000139-002-012-00001/Default.aspx.

Now a word on meditation. Or should that be,
not a word on meditation! Meditation is another
way to connect with your Higher Self.

Bestselling author Eckhart Tolle once quipped
that the world needs peace, not saving. I agree.
So, where does peace begin? As the song goes,
"Let there be peace on earth and let it begin with
me". That's the best place. It's really the only
place. If it's not in ourselves then how can we be
peacemakers (Matt 5:9) as Jesus called us to be? I
don't know about you but I could go for a world
without war!

To stop the warring in ourselves we first have to stop fighting ourselves and just listen and be at peace and accept ourselves.

Too often we find ourselves as "human doings" instead of "human beings". In fact, we're neither, really. We're divine beings having a human experience. But, it's a good reminder that it's more about being, being God, being still, being real.

So, go ahead, make that connection, whether by faith, prayer or meditation. It's all good!

HAHA!

What did the Yogi say when he walked into the Pizza Parlor?

"Make me one with everything."

When the Yogi got the pizza, he gave the proprietor a $20 bill. The proprietor pocketed the bill. The Yogi said "Don't I get change?"

The proprietor said, "Change must come from within."

Word Scramble!

rryePa _______________

nitedotiMa _______________

haitF _______________

tecconeRn hitw odG! _______________________

CH 10: Are you good looking or What?

Mirror, mirror on the wall, who is the fairest of them all? "I AM!" you can say, and it's true, because God is in you!

As you grow up, you start to think about appearances more. How do I look? Am I good looking? Do I make the cut? Do I fit in? Do I look okay? Well, I'm here to tell you that you look awesome! How do I know when I haven't even seen you? Well, it's because your real beauty is inside. And we all have it!

This spiritual beauty is your true beauty. This includes your character. What's character? No, it's not a cartoon character on your TV! It means virtuous behavior. And no, that's not stuffy or out of reach. It's sacred. It's Godly (which basically means, like-God and you can't get any better than that!)

True qualities worth reaching for include honesty, integrity (look that one up in the dictionary!), kindness, being truthful, honor,

If you don't look perfect, don't worry, it's not you anyhow. It's just a body you're using for this life. You, yourself, are a shining spirit of God's love!

thoughtfulness, courage and unselfishness. There
are so many qualities I could go on and on. In a
way, it doesn't really matter which one you
choose, just as long as you choose one (or
more) and really, truly, become that quality in
all ways. It'll really change your life when
you do.

Having trouble deciding? I just stuck
with "love." It's pretty universal.

When you look at body image from a
spiritual perspective, it changes things.
It's no longer your body (it's God's). Besides, it's
no longer you either (your true identity is a spirit,
first and foremost).

A lot of people talk about "my body" and that
makes sense. It's certainly no one else's and it's
the one we've controlled ever since we were

conceived. The Christian Bible
talks about us being the
"temple of God". So, what is a
temple anyhow? It's a place of
worship. Who is worshipped
there? God. By whatever name
you prefer. It doesn't matter if
you call God, God, as most
Christian folks do. Or whether you like to think of
this Creator as Universal Love. Or whatever else.

God knows who you're talking to! So, why are you the temple of God? Simple. God's in you! (See Chapter 1.)

So, you are alive and God is alive in you and actually, you are kind of one and the same. Since, after all, God is where you came from and what you are destined to follow and grow into. It gives you a new sense of self-esteem. God Self-esteem.

Who cares what you look like when God's inside of you and that's who you truly are? Now, you can make yourself look good and that's a good idea. After all, God likes being in the earth and he/she needs a body to function through – that means you! We can look after ourselves by eating healthy foods, getting fresh air and exercise, maintaining a healthy weight, keeping clean, feeding our minds wholesome stuff, staying positive and pure. We can even do little things like choosing what we wear to reflect who we truly are.

We can consecrate our life to God and our bodies to God. This doesn't mean your life is going to be boring. Far from it! It means God knows you desire to be his/her instrument. God's going to use you because you've asked for it by your choice. And that's important, because God gave us choice in the beginning. Just another example of how God wanted to make you like himself/herself!

So, no matter what the world says or holds up as an image, you look great, you are great and your body (which actually isn't yours) is a really awesome temple of God. So, just relax. All you've got to do is let God in, I mean, out.

EXERCISE: Draw yourself in the
mirror as God sees you!

CH 11: Music on your Spiritual Path

Have you ever felt the powerful sound of a piece of music tug at your heart and soul as you soak in its rhythm and sound, nodding, moving, dancing, crying, whatever, to the sound, the wonderful sound...of music?

Music. It's powerful stuff. In long bygone days, only the most spiritually advanced were allowed to dabble in this sacred and powerful art form. Music is made of sound. But what is sound?

Sound is waves of energy that our ears pick up and our brain interprets. Sometimes we don't realize its power.

Have you ever seen someone vocalize a sound that is the right pitch suddenly break a drinking glass? If not, check it out on YouTube! It's pretty amazing.

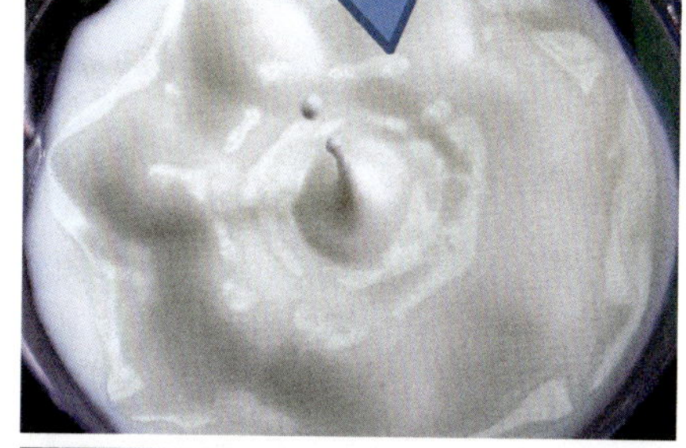

Over a hundred years ago, a guy by the name of Hans Jenny came up with this cool device that plays sound through a metal plate containing sand. Through vibration, the sound aligns the sand into a form on the metal plate. As the pitch is turned higher and higher the pattern will suddenly shift, literally flipping the sand into a new pattern, much like a kaleidoscope.[7]

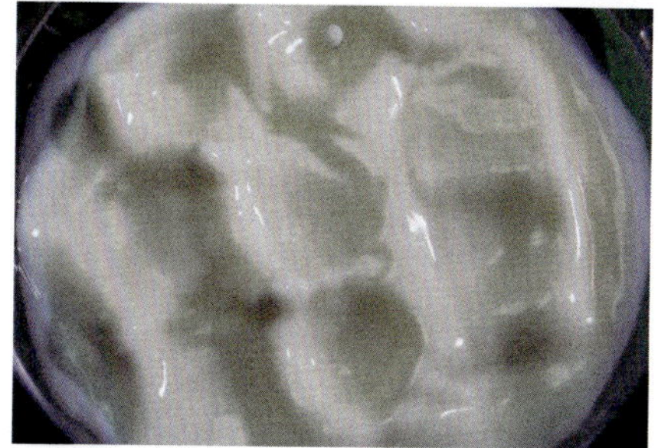

In other fascinating experiments viewable on YouTube, you can see how changes in pitch, chanting or singing create a pattern in the sand and how

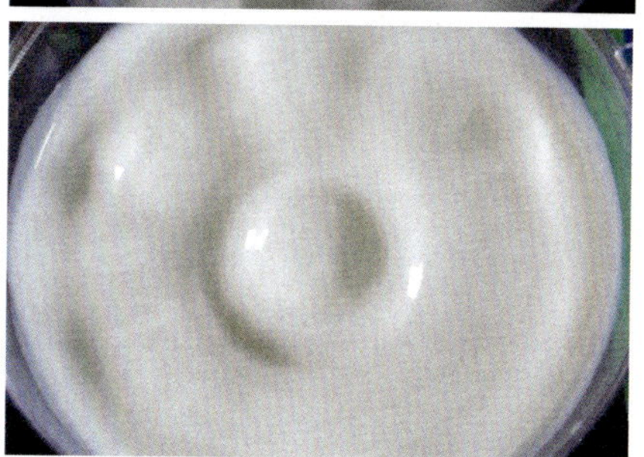

---

[7] "Hans Jenny – Cymatics," Uploaded on October 16, 2009, https://youtu.be/W6PSA5bYTxs. Also check out this TED talk "Evan Grant: Making sound visible through cymatics," Uploaded on September 9, 2009, https://youtu.be/CsjV1gjBMbQ.

the shapes suddenly reform when the sound changes.[8]

It's fascinating when you think that sound could shape matter. We don't really think of it, but maybe we should! After all, we read in the Bible that, "In the beginning was the Word, and the Word was with God, and the Word was God… and without him was not anything made that was made." (John 1:1,3)

That's no small statement! Nothing was made without sound! Which is one way you could interpret the text. Especially since God apparently created the heavens and earth through speaking, "let there be light!" (Gen 1:3) and so on. Actually, if you really want to stretch

---

[8] See for example "Tonoscope, Sound in form", Published on July 13, 2014, https://youtu.be/_MN1o8L9kJ4, and "Sacred Chant Recorded Inside the Great Pyramid The Language 'OF LIGHT'," Published on August 14, 2012, https://youtu.be/lgzd1yh5wL8. There are many more.

your mind, how about this? God SANG the command.[9] I bet you never thought of that one!

Sound has been around for a long time….and it's still a major part of our lives. Yet we take it for granted and just think of it as some form of entertainment.

You could probably guess that music can influence your heart rate and breathing, even blood pressure. Just think of the music during a movie where something is about to happen. It wouldn't have half the impact if there was no music!

So maybe music is more than just entertainment! Actually, it's behavior modification! Have you ever noticed what kind of music is generally played in the subway, train stations, airports and places like that? I'll give you a clue, it's not rap! And it's not pop either. It's usually classical music of some sort. Why? Because of the effect on your mood. It just doesn't inspire gangs to get out their graffiti spray to the sound of Mozart's

---

[9] Lewis, David Christopher. "The Seven Octaves of Vibration: Let Your Keynote be Harmony" by God Harmony. The Hearts Center.
http://www.heartscenter.org/TeachingsBlogs/HeartStreamsandDiscourses/The HeartStreamsDatabase/tabid/66/afn/110805-God%20Harmony-000182-010-002-00001/Default.aspx.

Eine kleine Nachtmusik. It could also be, as someone humorously pointed out, that those types just leave the area because they don't like the music. Either way, it works.

You see, music is powerful. Through music, you channel. What are you channeling? Is it God and your Higher Self or is it the self-gratification of the human self?

Every artist gets their music from somewhere. The good and bad ones admit this. It either comes from above or below. Besides where it's inspired from, it also comes through the musician's consciousness. So, take a check and see if you find the lives of those whose music you listen to inspiring or not.

Everything we hear plays through our mind and eventually ends up in our subconscious, programming us from within. Do you choose to listen to music that helps you become your personal best and that helps you attune to God?

Our lives are a choice. Let's make it a conscious one!

So, what kind of music can help you do that? Well, the second part of the question is easy. Music that can help attune you to God is often devotional. Traditional Christian hymns, Bhajans (Indian religious songs), Buddhist mantras, Gregorian chants and other holy songs of many faiths and traditions may all do this.

Now, what about the first part of the question. What can help you become your personal best? Well, first of all, let's define it. We're talking about music that helps you connect with all that IS. Music that helps you tune into the perfection, beauty and intelligence of the Universe. Music that raises you in consciousness. Sound deep? It is! That is music that helps you become your best, because after all, your true Self is God and God is beauty, perfection, harmony, joy and peace.

If your music reflects that, way to go! Literally. If not, maybe it's time for some self-reflection on what you really desire from life.

While you're sitting with that idea, let's lighten up a little. Did you know that cats going under surgery show signs of being calm and relaxed to classical music?[10] Or that dogs' behavior calms down and shows less unrest while listening to classical music?[11] Or that classical music can help cows relax, thus producing more milk?[12] Or that chicken's eggs become more plentiful and larger under the positive sound of classical music?[13]

Hey, even plants prefer classical music![14] Lots of different studies show plants either growing taller, healthier or even towards the speakers of the preferred music! Now that can't be the

[10] "Cats Prefer Classical Music When They're Having Surgery," The Huffington Post, April 2, 2015, http://www.huffingtonpost.com/2015/04/02/cats-classical-music_n_6990372.html.
[11] "Study: Classical music de-stresses dogs," CBS News, November 6, 2012, http://www.cbsnews.com/news/study-classical-music-de-stresses-dogs/.
[12] "Rock On: Classical Music a Favorite Among Dairy Cows," Dairy Good, April 4, 2013, https://dairygood.org/content/2013/rock-on-classical-music-a-favorite-among-dairy-cows.
[13] "Chickens mad for Mozart produce bigger, heavier eggs," CBC News, May 2, 2014, http://www.cbc.ca/news/canada/nova-scotia/chickens-mad-for-mozart-produce-bigger-heavier-eggs-1.2630194.
[14] "How Do Plants React to Classical Music?" eHow, no date, http://www.ehow.com/how-does_5421613_do-plants-react-classical-music.html.

placebo effect where it's all in the listener's mind!

So, going back to the cats and dogs, do you have any idea why they might be more likely to be less relaxed with the rock/pop stuff compared to classical? Both types can relax you or wind you up but it's deeper than that.

Our body has rhythms. Take your heartbeat, for example. Without that we would be dead. It's a constant, steady rhythm and one that we appreciate being there.

When you have a beat that is similar to the heart beat it reinforces your heart's function and harmony. The waltz is said to be the most similar to the heart beat as far as music goes.

When you have something that tends to go against the natural, expected rhythm, that's syncopation. Although some classical pieces contain syncopation, it is the signature of rock and roll, having that drum beat underlying the song.

So, this beat is actually not the best for your body, as plants and animals affirm.

Here's something funny. Some psychologists and a composer got together and rearranged human music to suit cats' heartbeats and frequencies and they loved it: "the cats couldn't get enough, rubbing their faces against the speakers in approval."[15] Are cats smarter than us that they know what is good for them?

Anyhow, let's look at the good side of music. Do you know that a Greek philosopher way back in 500 BC proposed the idea of the music of the spheres? I guess others might have proposed the idea too, but he's the oldest, most famous guy we have on record about this. So, what are these musical spheres anyhow?

Actually, they are the planets. According to this theory, each planet emits a tone or hum. Now what do you think it would sound like to hear all the planets and the sun all making their own unique sounds? It may be that this is too high/low for human ears to hear. Perhaps our

---

[15] "Your cat thinks your taste in music sucks and now scientists have proved why," Mirror, March 28, 2015, http://www.mirror.co.uk/usvsth3m/your-cat-thinks-your-taste-5418497.

dogs are hearing it! Or in any case, angels. Still, through The Hearts Center it has been said,

"...one day you will even hear the turning of worlds. Yes, you will hear the music of the spheres."[16]

– Arcturus, May 2, 2009

Now, that's just our solar system. What about the galaxies unlimited throughout our mighty universe? That's got to be one humongous, powerful symphony of sound when you add them all altogether!

What's even more interesting is, why stop there? Why can't everything have its own sound or hum or vibration? Including you! You have a keynote, a melody or tune that is just you, the signature of your Divine Self. And maybe, as we grow

---

[16] Lewis, David Christopher. "A Bedtime Story from Our Godparents, the Elohim" by Arcturus. The Hearts Center. http://www.heartscenter.org/TeachingsBlogs/HeartStreamsandDiscourses/The HeartStreamsDatabase/tabid/66/afn/090502-Arcturus-000139-002-012-00001/Default.aspx.

spiritually over time – although time doesn't exist for God – we will eventually have a more complex symphony that just gets more grand and magnificent.

So, if you're wondering, here are a few famous pieces that are said to be keynotes of certain masters. You see, it's like I said. Music can be inspired from above or below. Everything comes from somewhere.

Ode to Joy – Gautama Buddha

Finlandia – Ancient of Days (Sanat Kumara)

Joy to the World – Jesus Christ

Radetzky March – Godfre

Navy Hymn (aka Eternal Father) – Archangel Michael

Hungarian Rhapsody No. 15 (aka Rakoczy March) – Divine Director

Pomp and Circumstance – El Morya

Holy, Holy, Holy – Archangels

Triumphal March – Ascension flame

Brahms Lullaby – Archangel Uriel

Here's something else. You don't have to listen to music. You can make your own. It doesn't matter if you can't play an instrument. Your voice is a powerful instrument!

We can charge our voice with the love of our hearts and ask the angels to sing through us as we sing uplifting, pure and joyful songs.

Some people think it's old fashioned to imagine that angels sing in heaven and that they have much more practical work to do. While that may be true of some bands of angels, others are constantly pouring out this stream of glory and praise to God on high. It must be magnificent to hear. I look forward to hearing it!

On rare occasions you find these angelic songs becoming physical when someone has the experience of hearing a glimmer of heavenly sounds.

Even on YouTube there is the story of some group that was recording their worship song and when they played it back it had high, long notes, sung by many, many voices. Check it out if you're interested![17] There are others as well.

We covered a lot of things in this chapter and there are so many more we didn't even touch on. You get the gist of it. Music is powerful.

---

[17] "Angels singing caught on tape (Updated) Improved sound quality and lyrics to the mystery solo," Published on November 25, 2012, https://youtu.be/wxgfnEkxkMI.

A conversation in one of the heavenly regions...

Take your music to test!

1. How do you feel like moving when you hear the piece?
2. Ask yourself, how would you feel playing this piece of music for Jesus or Buddha?
3. Do a music fast. Avoid music for a week then listen to the piece again. Your response may surprise you!

Conclusion

So, we've come to the end of our time together. Or have we? I'm really in everything and everywhere you are. And you are really in me.

I hope you've begun to think about <u>Who are you?</u> and <u>Why am I here?</u> and why <u>Your actions matter.</u> Maybe you've started to realize that your soul has <u>Been there, done that!</u> longer than you think. But that's okay, because <u>You are a powerful spiritual being</u> just as <u>Heaven has powerful spiritual beings too!</u> I'm glad you've started to consider if <u>you'd like to become an Ascended master.</u> It helps get you thinking on the right track since the life <u>Tests are coming!</u> Have you <u>Got connection?</u> Just relax and know that the answer to <u>Are you good looking or what?</u> is always yes, since God is all that is real about you.

And finally, a key to your spiritual path, yes, a key, ha-ha, is <u>Music on your spiritual path.</u> Was that a C note or D note? Anyhow, it doesn't matter. What matters is that you grow spiritually, that you grow as a person, that you realize God in you and in all life.

So long pal! See you 'round in the great cycle of life!

Just Remember…

Life is good. God is good. You are good. Even when things seem convoluted or messed up or upside down, it will work out. All things work together for those who serve God. Keep on keeping on and uncovering the fun mysteries the universe has in store for you. The fun is just beginning!

You'll need a mirror to read me!

ANSWerS

CH 1: Who are you? A journey in God-Self Discovery

"You are made of God stuff!"

CH 2: So, why am I here? What do I do with my life?

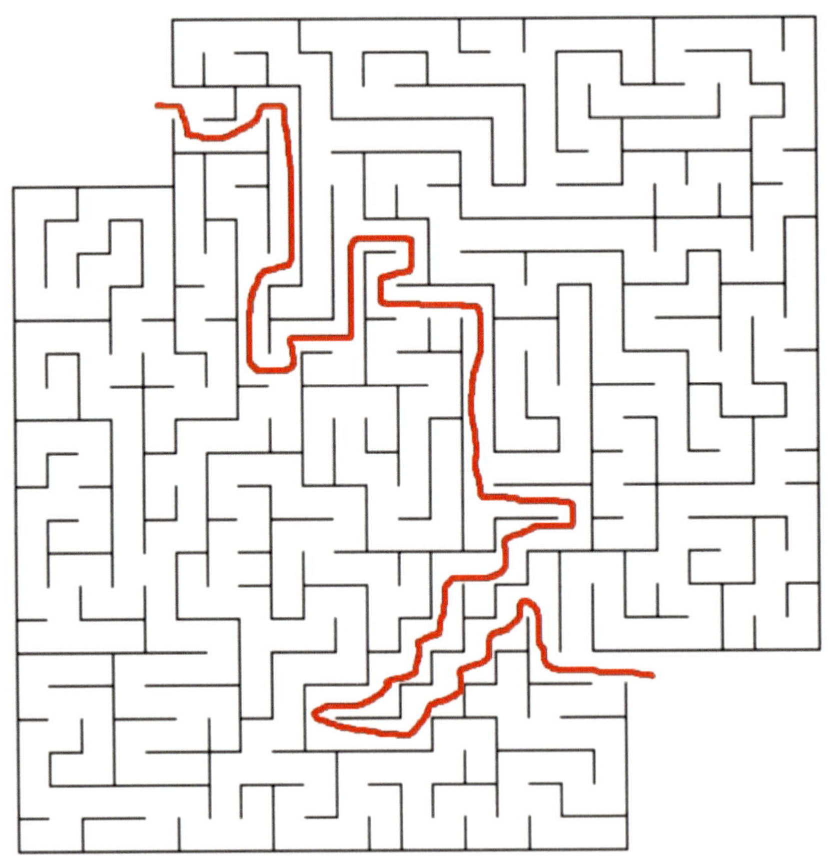

Did you complete your treasure map?

CH 3: Your actions matter – here's why, and what to do about it!

a) "Fruits"

CH 4: Been there, done that!

"I didn't believe in reincarnation at your age, either."

CH 5: You are a powerful spiritual being

What did you imagine?

CH 6: Heaven has powerful spiritual beings too!

```
+ + + + + + + + G + K K B + + + + Y S
+ + + + L E A H P A R + U R I E L + + R A
+ + + + + Y V + + B + + + A I + + + J A I
+ + + + R + T + + R + + + H N S + O + M N
+ + + O + + T P + I + + + M + Y H + + R T
+ I M H S K A L + E + + + A S N I N + E T
A L P H A D S P A L L A S A T H E N A H H
E + + A R F A K E D E Z I H C L E M K T E
R + + E A + R D I V I N E D I R E C T O R
F + P + S + J M + + T B + D S + I O + M E
D I + + V + A + + G A + + U + R M N + R S
O + + + A I V R E P H + S B T N U F + A E
G + M O T H E R T E R E S A + A H U + A O
+ + L R I N M I R S J + P M + H T C + M F
A G E M O A S C + + U T + A + O U I + + L
+ Y A C I T U + + + N H + T + H K U + + I
A + H N + L + + + I + + T U + C + S + + S
+ V C + E S A N A T K U M A R A U + + + I
+ + I S + + + S + + + + G R H + Z + + E
+ + M H + + + + A M A Z O N I A + + C + U
+ + + + S + + + N O R T A T E M Z + + O X
```

CH 7: So you'd like to become an Ascended master?

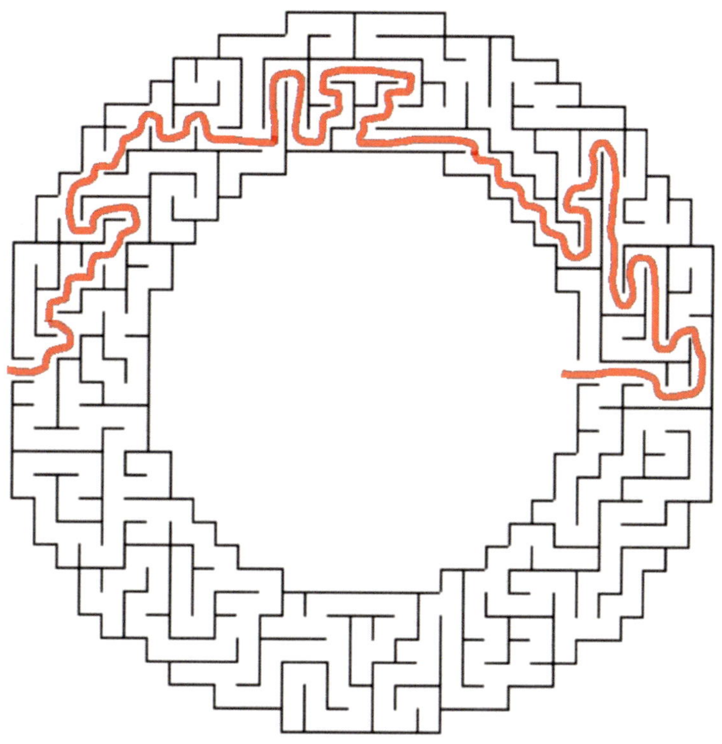

CH 8: Tests are coming – and I don't mean school tests!

Did you figure out what it means to be true to yourself?

CH 9: Got connection?

rryePa – Prayer

nitedotiMa – Meditation

haitF – Faith

tecconeRn hitw odG! – Reconnect with God!

CH 10: Are you good looking or what?

Did you draw yourself in the mirror?

CH 11: Music on your spiritual path

Did you test your music out?

Acknowledgments

A sincere thank you to:

My God, the source of all wisdom and truth.

Beloved Meta, for your idea and inspiration for this book.

My husband, Charles, for your support always and in every way.

David and The Hearts Center, for your kind assistance in making this book a reality.

Claire, for your helpful advice and experience with publishing details.

Denis and all of your team, for your expert help in turning this manuscript into a real book.

About the Author

Serena Gaefke lives with her husband and three children in southern Arizona. She is passionate about early education, spritual education of the heart, and living a spiritual life.

Contact Serena by email at:
spirituality4kids@heartscenter.org

Made in the USA
Middletown, DE
05 October 2018